info buzz

Transport

Izzi Howell

W
FRANKLIN WATTS
LONDON • SYDNEY

Franklin Watts

First published in Great Britain in 2019 by The Watts Publishing Group

Copyright © The Watts Publishing Group, 2019

Produced for Franklin Watts by
White-Thomson Publishing Ltd
www.wtpub.co.uk

ISBN (HB): 978 1 4451 6479 3
ISBN (PB): 978 1 4451 6480 9

Credits
Series Editor: Izzi Howell
Series Designer: Rocket Design (East Anglia) Ltd
Designer: Clare Nicholas
Literacy Consultant: Kate Ruttle
Historical Consultant: Philip Parker

The publisher would like to thank the following for permission to reproduce their pictures: Alamy: colobusyeti. co.uk 11t, Oote Boe 18; Getty: Culture Club cover, BeyondImages title page and 12, Hulton Collection 4, schlol 5t, spooh 5b, Michael SERRAILLIER/Gamma-Rapho 7t, Hulton-Deutsch Collection/Corbis 8, atlantic-kid 9 and 17t, Fox Photos 10, Harry Todd/Fox Photos/Hulton Archive 13t, FPG 14, whitemay 19; NASA: 20, David Scott 21; Shutterstock: Ungor 6 and 22, Monkey Business Images 7b, Ceri Breeze 11b, Tupungato 13b, Peter James Sampson 15, Everett Historical 16, Ditty_about_summer 17b.

Every attempt has been made to clear copyright. Should there be any inadvertent omission please apply to the publisher for rectification.

Printed in China

Franklin Watts
An imprint of
Hachette Children's Group
Part of The Watts Publishing Group
Carmelite House
50 Victoria Embankment
London EC4Y 0DZ

An Hachette UK Company
www.hachette.co.uk
www.franklinwatts.co.uk

All words in **bold** appear in the glossary on page 23.

Contents

Then and now

We use transport to travel from one place to another. Cars, buses and trains are all types of transport.

Horse-drawn carriages were used as transport in the past. They aren't used often today.
▼

1900s

DISTRICT RAILWAY. BLACKFRIARS S

EW MINUTES.

BOOKING OFFICE

1930s

windscreen ------•

Transport has changed over time. Some types of transport looked different in the past.

▲
In the past, cars had smaller windscreens.

windscreen

today

5

Bicycles

Some of the first bicycles were made in **Victorian** times. Some Victorian bicycles looked different to **modern** bicycles.

This Victorian bicycle is called a penny farthing. Its front wheel is much larger than its back wheel. ▼

Victorian times

Bicycles have been **popular** with adults and children since Victorian times. People ride to work or school.

1970s

These children are practising turning a corner in a cycling lesson. ▶

◀ This family are riding their bicycles together for fun.

today

Can you ride a bicycle? Where do you go on your bicycle?

7

Cars

In the 1900s, people began to buy and drive cars. Cars were very expensive. Only a few rich people had cars.

▼ The first cars didn't have hard roofs.

How do you think it would feel to travel in a car without a roof?

1920s

Over time, more and more people were able to buy cars. Today, many people travel by car every day.

There weren't as many cars on the streets in the 1960s as there are today.

1960s

Buses

The first buses were carriages pulled by horses. **Passengers** sat inside or on top of the carriage.

1900s

These horse-drawn buses are **double-decker.** ▼

Later, buses with **engines** started to be used. They were faster than horse-drawn buses.

The name or the number on the front of the bus tells people where the bus is going. ▶

1970s

today

◀ Some modern buses are very long. They have more seats for passengers inside.

Trains

Many railways were built
in Victorian times. This made it
easier for people to move around.
Trains also transported food,
materials and objects to sell.

Until the 1950s and
1960s, all trains
were powered by
steam. The steam
came out of the
top of the engine. ▼

The first underground trains were also built in Victorian times. People still move around many cities by underground train today.

Underground trains travel through tunnels. ▶

1960s

◀ **People sit and stand on underground trains.**

Where have you travelled to by train?

today

Trams

Trams are trains that run on **rails** through the streets. They transport people around towns and cities.

Trams sometimes shared the streets with other types of transport.
▼

Victorian times

tram rails

tram

Which other types of transport can you see in this photo?

Some modern cities have trams. Trams can carry more passengers than cars or buses.

▲ People wait for trams at tram stops.

15

Aeroplanes

The first aeroplane flight was in 1903. The first aeroplanes were made from wood. They didn't have a roof or walls.

The pilot lay down in the centre of the aeroplane. ▼

1900s

pilot

Later, large aeroplanes were made from metal. Many people could travel inside.

Over time, people began to travel by aeroplane to faraway places on holiday or for work. ▼

1960s

AEROMARITIME

AIR FRANCE

today

Have you ever travelled by aeroplane? Where did you go?

Ships

Before aeroplanes became affordable, people in the UK could only travel to and from other countries in ships. Travelling by ship was slow.

▼ Large ships carried people across the sea to other countries. Going to other countries was expensive and unusual.

1930s

People still travel by ship today. Some people go on holiday on cruise ships.

Can you think of some other ways to travel across water?

Ferries travel back and forth between two places. They transport people and sometimes cars. ▼

today

Space

In the 1960s, **astronauts** went into space for the first time. They travelled in **spacecraft**.

This spacecraft is taking off. A powerful rocket is making it move upward.
▼

1970s

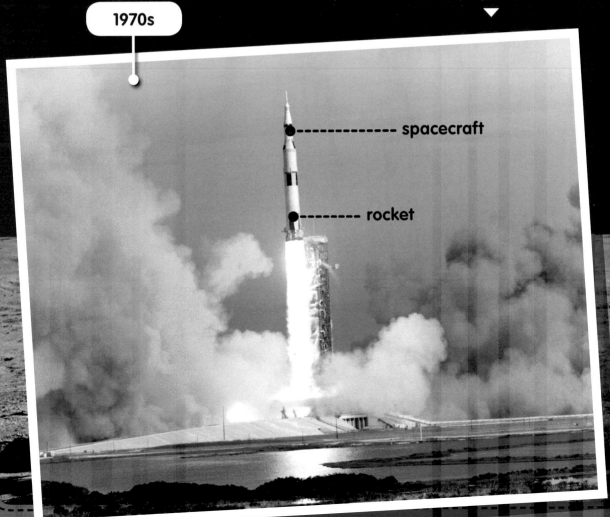

spacecraft

rocket

In 1969, the first astronauts walked on the Moon. Later, other astronauts explored the Moon in Moon **rovers**.

The rover was like a car.

1970s

Moon rover

Quiz

Test how much you remember.

Check your answers on page 24.

1 What is a penny farthing?

2 Which animal pulled the first buses?

3 When were the first underground trains built?

4 What are trams?

5 What were the first aeroplanes made from?

6 When did astronauts travel into space for the first time?

Glossary

astronaut – someone who travels into space

double-decker – a bus with two levels where people can sit

engine – the part of a vehicle that makes it move

horse-drawn carriage – a vehicle with wheels that is pulled by horses

materials – things used to make other objects

modern – describes something from today

passenger – someone who is travelling in a vehicle, but not driving it

pilot – someone who flies an aeroplane

popular – liked by many people

rail – a metal track that trains and trams run along

rover – a vehicle that can move over rough surfaces

spacecraft – a vehicle used for travel in space

steam – the gas produced when water boils

Victorian – the years from 1837 to 1901 in Britain, when Queen Victoria ruled the country

Index

Answers:

1: A Victorian bicycle with a large front wheel; 2: Horses; 3: Victorian times; 4: Trains that run on rails through the streets; 5: Wood; 6: 1960s

Teaching notes:

Children who are reading Book Band Purple or above should be able to enjoy this book with some independence. Other children will need more support.

Before you share the book:

- Ask children what they think 'transport' means. Agree on a shared definition that involves the idea of taking someone or something from one place to another.
- Make a class list of all the different types of transport you can think of.

While you share the book:

- Help children to read some of the more unfamiliar words.
- Talk about the questions. Encourage children to make links between their own experiences and the information in the book.

- Discuss the pictures, particularly the older pictures, identifying what is the same and what is different between transport in the past and now.

After you have shared the book:

- Ask children to ask their parents and grandparents about transport from when they were younger. Encourage children to find images of cars their parents/ grandparents may recall.
- Give each group of children pairs of pictures of a vehicle from the past and a comparable one today. Challenge them to list as many similarities and differences as they can.
- Ask children to think about the future. Have they seen cartoons, films or images showing ideas for transport in the future? Ask them to draw and label their own ideas.
- Work through the free activity sheets at www.hachetteschools.co.uk

History

978 1 4451 6477 9

Then and now
Getting to school
Learning
Writing
Classrooms
Uniform
School dinners
Sports
Playtime

978 1 4451 6449 6

Then and now
Getting to the beach
Towns
Beach clothes
Food
Beach toys
Entertainment
Piers
Buildings

978 1 4451 6476 2

Then and now
Dolls
Soft toys
Trains, boats and cars
Board games
Puzzles
Building blocks
Computer games
Playing outdoors

978 1 4451 6479 3

Then and now
Carriages
Trains
Cars
Planes
Buses
Ships
Bicycles
Space

Religion

Christianity
978 1 4451 5962 1
Hinduism
978 1 4451 5964 5
Islam
978 1 4451 5968 3
Judaism
978 1 4451 5966 9

History

Neil Armstrong
978 1 4451 5948 5
Queen Elizabeth II
978 1 4451 5886 0
Queen Victoria
978 1 4451 5950 8
Tim Berners-Lee
978 1 4451 5952 2

People who help us

Doctors
978 1 4451 6493 9
Firefighters
978 1 4451 6489 2
Paramedics
978 1 4451 6495 3
Police Officers
978 1 4451 6491 5

Countries

Argentina
978 1 4451 5958 4
India
978 1 4451 5960 7
Japan
978 1 4451 5956 0
The United Kingdom
978 1 4451 5954 6

FRANKLIN
WATTS